Surviving Disaster:
Real Life Tales of Survival and Resilience

Surviving the 2011 JAPANESE EARTHQUAKE and TSUNAMI

Kira Freed

rosen publishing's
rosen central

New York

Published in 2016 by The Rosen Publishing Group, Inc.
29 East 21st Street, New York, NY 10010

Developed and produced for Rosen by BlueApple*Works* Inc.

Art Director: T.J. Choleva

Managing Editor for BlueApple*Works*: Melissa McClellan
Designer: Joshua Avramson
Photo Research: Jane Reid
Editor: Marcia Abramson

This book was reviewed by Kenji Tateiwa, Manager, Nuclear Power Programs, Tokyo Electric Power Company, Washington Office

Photo Credits: Creative Commons: Hikosaemon (p. 13); p. 21; Mitsukuni Sato (p. 26); Daniel Pierce (p. 29); DVIDSHUB
(p. 31); Keystone Press: © Mainichi Newspaper (cover, p. 22); © Hitoshi Yamada (p. 4); © Kyodo (p. 10); © Feng Wuyong (p. 14); © Tohankoku (p. 34); © Koichi Kamoshida (p. 39); © Hitoshi Yamada (p. 45); Public Domain: U.S. Air Force photo/Staff Sgt. Samuel Morse (title page); United States Geological Survey (p. 7); U.S. Navy photo/Lance Cpl. Garry Welch (p. 17); U.S. Air Force photo/Staff Sgt. Robin Stanchak (p. 25); U.S. Navy photo (p. 31, back cover); Shutterstock.com: © 2nix Studio (p. 8); Thinkstock: © Brad Calkins (p. 18); © Stocktrek Images (p. 40)

Library of Congress Cataloging-in-Publication Data

Freed, Kira.

Surviving the 2011 Japanese earthquake and tsunami/Kira Freed.—First edition.

    pages cm.—(Surviving disaster)

Includes bibliographical references and index.

ISBN 978-1-4994-3645-7 (library bound)—ISBN 978-1-4994-3647-1 (pbk.)—
ISBN 978-1-4994-3648-8 (6-pack)

1. Tohoku Earthquake and Tsunami, Japan, 2011—Juvenile literature. 2. Emergency management—Japan—Tohoku Region—Juvenile literature. I. Title.

HV600 2011 .T64 F74 2016

363.34'950952090512—dc23

2015002400

Contents

At least 1,500 earthquakes happen each year in Japan. A few cause damage like this, but most do not.

Chapter 1

Deadly Tremors

Most people think of the ground beneath our feet as a solid, stable surface. In fact, it's always on the move. Earth's crust is made up of tectonic plates—massive slabs of rock that fit together like puzzle pieces. Earth's mantle, which is located under the crust, is made up of hot, weak rock with the consistency of an extremely thick liquid. Heat from Earth's core creates **convection currents** that cause the hot rock to move very slowly. As the mantle moves, the tectonic plates above it also move. Geologists use special terms to describe the interactions of plates at their boundaries. Plates slide past each other at transform boundaries, they slide away from each other at divergent boundaries, and they slide toward each other at convergent boundaries.

Tectonic plates usually move very slowly, but sometimes they move in an instant. At transform boundaries, earthquakes can occur when two plates get stuck and then suddenly slip past each other. The energy radiates outward in every direction as seismic waves, which cause tremors to ripple through the ground far above.

Earthquakes can also take place along convergent boundaries. When an oceanic plate and a continental plate converge, the denser oceanic plate is thrust beneath the continental plate and into the mantle in a process called subduction. The boundary where the two plates meet is called a subduction zone. Earth's most powerful earthquakes occur at subduction zones because of the degree to which energy builds up before being released. These events are often referred to as **megathrust** earthquakes.

Many earthquakes are so small that they are hardly noticeable, but others are huge and **devastating**. A large earthquake can cause buildings to crumble, bridges to collapse, and underground pipes to break. It can also trigger landslides and open up large fissures in the ground. An additional perilous consequence of many large earthquakes, especially megathrust earthquakes, is tsunamis—series of ocean waves often caused by violent shifts of the seafloor as a result of earthquakes. (Volcanic eruptions and underwater landslides can also cause tsunamis.) Not all earthquakes on the seafloor result in tsunamis, and not all tsunamis are perilous. However, some grow taller as they move toward land and turn into enormous walls of water by the time they reach the shore. A tsunami can destroy coastal communities in an instant and also travel far inland. An extremely powerful tsunami can also travel across an ocean and cause destruction thousands of miles away.

Mount St. Helens is an active volcano in Washington state. The volcano erupted on May 18, 1980, triggering a strong earthquake. Fifty-seven people died in the volcano disaster.

Mount Fuji is a distinctive feature of the geography of Japan. It is the highest mountain in Japan and an active volcano. Mount Fuji last erupted in 1707, after a powerful 8.7 earthquake.

Japan is located on the Ring of Fire, a horseshoe-shaped area around the edges of the Pacific Ocean and the site of a great deal of seismic activity. The Pacific Plate—Earth's fastest-moving plate—is subducting beneath several other tectonic plates along deep ocean trenches. This process has been generating earthquakes, along with volcanic eruptions and tsunamis, for millions of years.

Scientists are not sure just how many active volcanoes there are today, but it could be more than a thousand. About ten percent of these are in Japan, and more than twenty percent of the world's earthquakes happen there. Japan experiences at least 1,500 quakes per year, though most of them are minor.

With its long history of earthquakes and tsunamis, Japan has learned to be in a constant state of readiness. A seismic network with over 1,200 sensors monitors land and seafloor movement, computer simulations predict the likelihood of tsunamis, and warning and **evacuation** protocols are in place. Children learn safety measures, and schools regularly conduct disaster drills. Buildings are constructed to sway, and a system of seawalls protects over one-third of Japan's coastline.

Measuring Earthquakes

For many years, scientists used the Richter Scale to measure the strength, or magnitude, of an earthquake. They now use a more accurate measure—the Moment Magnitude Scale. Instruments called seismographs record the amplitude of seismic waves during an earthquake. The number assigned to an earthquake represents its seismic moment, or total energy. Earthquakes too small to be perceived may measure 1.0 on the scale. Earthquakes measuring 9.0 and above can cause complete destruction and significant loss of life.

The City of Natori was one of the many coastal cities devastated by massive tsunami waves after a powerful quake in 2011.

Chapter 2
Deluge of 2011

On the afternoon of March 11, 2011, a magnitude 9.0 megathrust earthquake struck off the north-eastern coast of Honshu, Japan's main island. The earthquake's **epicenter** was eighty-one miles (130 km) east of Sendai, a city of over one million people.

The earthquake caused fires in a number of cities as well as widespread destruction of buildings, roads, railway lines, power lines, and water and sewer systems. In addition, the earthquake triggered a series of powerful tsunami waves that devastated much of Honshu's eastern coastline and traveled up to six miles (ten km) inland in some places. The tsunami waves also caused major **meltdowns** at Fukushima Daiichi Nuclear Power Station, located fifty-three miles (eighty-five km) south of Sendai along the coast.

Confirmed deaths from the earthquake and tsunami totaled more than 15,800, and almost 2,600 are still missing. The majority of casualties were drownings resulting from the tsunami waves. More than 1.2 million buildings were damaged or completely destroyed. Estimates of property damage were as high as $309 billion. Japan and its people are still recovering from the events of March 11, 2011.

Earthquake 9.0

On March 9, 2011—two days before the massive mega thrust earthquake—Japan experienced a 7.2 earthquake whose epicenter was twenty-five miles (forty km) south of the March 11 quake. The 7.2 earthquake was followed by three large aftershocks, each measuring over 6.0, as well as small tsunami waves that reached a maximum height of two feet (sixty cm). The March 9 earthquake was just large enough to fool people in the area into thinking no larger one would follow soon after. To everyone's surprise, the 7.2 earthquake and its aftershocks turned out to be foreshocks of the 9.0 earthquake that occurred two days later.

The Tohoku earthquake, as it is now referred to, struck at 2:46 p.m. local time on March 11. Its **hypocenter** was approximately twenty miles (thirty-two km) below the surface of the Pacific Ocean. When the earthquake struck, the Pacific Plate subducted under the continental plate on which Japan's islands are situated. The two plates moved horizontally by as much as 164 feet (fifty meters), the largest fault movement ever recorded along a **fault zone** up to 310 miles (500 km) in length. Vertically, an area of the sea-floor roughly the size of Connecticut was lifted by thirty feet (nine meters) or more. This vertical shifting, which **displaced** a vast amount of water, caused the tsunami.

The Tohoku earthquake shook for six minutes and moved the island of Honshu eastward by up to about sixteen feet (five meters). It was the strongest recorded earthquake to ever hit Japan and Earth's fourth-strongest earthquake since 1900, when instruments were first used to record the strength of earthquakes. In the weeks following the earthquake, the area experienced hundreds of aftershocks, including two measuring at least 7.0. The earthquake was powerful enough to have an impact across the globe and be detected in space.

The earthquake caused widespread damage along Japan's coastline, including more than eighty fires. One, at the Cosmo oil refinery near Tokyo, sent plumes of black smoke high in the air and burned for ten days. More than a million buildings were destroyed or damaged. The region experienced loss of electric power, damage to roads and railway lines, and disruption to water and sewer systems. Fujinuma Dam, near Fukushima City, burst soon after the earthquake, releasing its entire reservoir.

People flooded the streets after the quake as offices and trains were evacuated in Japan's capital of Tokyo.

Though fires broke out as the city was badly shaken, Tokyo mostly escaped the disaster.

Survivor Account

Jide Obadina, a teacher, was at his gym in Tokyo's skyscraper district when the earthquake struck. As he was leaving the gym, he heard a roaring sound and saw things falling all around him. "That was when I ran for my life," he said. Obadina described his experience of the earthquake as similar to standing on a boat. He stated, "There is nothing more terrifying than being surrounded by huge buildings that could come down on your head. You could hear them creak and groan. I've been in earthquakes before but this was absolutely crazy. The strangest thing was how quiet everything was. All you could hear were sirens and smatterings of nervous chatter."

Liquid Wall of Destruction

The Tohoku earthquake caused considerable damage on its own, but the tsunami waves triggered by its seismic waves rippling through the seafloor resulted in unfathomable devastation. The first waves reached Japan's coastline less than an hour after the 9.0 earthquake struck.

When people think about a tsunami wave, they often imagine a towering arc of water similar to a "surfable" wave in Hawaii that breaks along the shore. In fact, only the largest tsunami waves have that appearance. Most—including the ones that hit Japan in 2011—come ashore as rapidly rising turbulent water, somewhat similar to the tide coming in but far faster. As the water continues to rise, it carries cars, boats, buildings, and a vast amount of debris, all of which fill the space between stationary objects at a relentless pace until nothing can move. People can quickly drown or get struck and killed by the moving **debris**. They can also be fooled by the lower water level after a tsunami wave and be caught by the next one.

A large majority of the lives lost on March 11, 2011, were caused by the tsunami waves rather than the earthquake. Many people thought they had escaped by reaching higher ground, only to find out that the water rose much higher and faster than expected.

Survivor Account

After the earthquake struck, Hiromitsu Shinkawa and his wife returned home to the town of Minamisoma to gather some of their belongings. That's when the tsunami hit. His wife was carried away by the water, but he managed to climb onto the roof of his house, which was then swept out to sea. For two days, Shinkawa drifted on the roof nine miles (fourteen km) from shore, waving a red cloth tied to a long stick to try to get someone's attention. Several ships and helicopters passed by without noticing him. Finally, a Japanese naval destroyer spotted him and sent a small boat to rescue him. He wept after being brought on board, saying, "I thought today was the last day of my life."

Along the coast, many tried to rescue people and were themselves caught in the next wave of incoming water. A large number of those who died were older people who couldn't move fast enough to escape the water.

The tsunami waves mainly **inundated** a long ribbon of coastline about 0.62 mile (one km) wide, but the damage reached as far inland as 6.2 miles (ten km) in several places. An area of land measuring roughly 200 square miles (518 km²)—almost as large as Chicago—was underwater. The maximum vertical height of water onshore above sea level, called run-up, was 128 feet (thirty-nine meters), at Miyako City.

Miyako, a port city, lost most of its fishing fleet in the tsunami, which devastated its economy.

Many coastal areas in Japan have concrete seawalls, some taller than thirty-five feet (eleven meters), for protection against tsunami waves. Controversy exists regarding their effectiveness.

Chapter 3
Early Warnings

Japan is located in one of the most seismically active parts of the world, and the country experiences frequent earthquakes and tsunamis. Extraordinary measures have been put in place to prepare for seismic events, minimize damage, and warn citizens in advance.

Approximately three-quarters of Japan's buildings are earthquake resistant. Many new buildings are constructed on top of base isolation pads. Made of rubber, lead, and steel, these devices allow a building to rest on a flexible surface that moves as the ground moves. Another device, called an energy dissipation unit, is a **hydraulic** cylinder embedded in a building's structure that expands and contracts as the building sways to reduce stress. All buildings in Japan are equipped with a device that immediately turns off the gas in the event of an earthquake.

The Earthquake Early Warning (EEW) system, established in 2007 by the Japan Meteorological Agency, is designed to warn people and reduce earthquake-related damage in a variety of ways. The EEW system announces a seismic event just after it is first detected, estimating its epicenter as well as expected arrival time so citizens have a few extra seconds—or more, depending on distance from the epicenter—to protect themselves. Tsunami warnings are also announced, although they take longer because they involve more complex calculations.

EEW alerts are sent to cell phones and pop up on television. A loud chime tone and message announce seismic events on radios. Special software allows computer users to receive EEW warnings via the Internet, and homes, offices, and schools also have standalone receivers.

The alerts allow railway workers to slow down trains and factory workers to stop assembly lines. Surgeons can stop delicate procedures, and workers can interrupt hazardous tasks. People can take cover, and drivers can pull off the road. The alerts also help people in schools and other gathering places evacuate safely.

Survivor Account

Nick Schneider, an American college professor, was on a high-speed train from Sendai to Tokyo when the earthquake struck. The train shuddered, billowed brown smoke, and made a great deal of noise as it quickly came to an emergency stop. Nick wrote, "The aftershocks kept coming, and coming, and coming. ... At first we thought it just meant a long time before we would start again, but then we came to realize how big the initial quake must have been. And that a stopped train safe in the countryside was the least of anyone's problems." After nine hours, buses rescued the train's passengers.

Early alerts helped railway workers to stop and evacuate thousands of trains safely.

Other safety precautions are in place as well. High-speed trains have a seismic early warning system that causes trains to stop automatically if they start moving faster than a certain speed. Many elevators, especially those in earthquake-prone regions and high-rise buildings, have seismic detectors; the first vibrations cause the elevators to return to the ground floor so people can leave. Nuclear power plants immediately shut down in the event of an earthquake.

These safety measures saved countless lives on March 11. Still, no one anticipated the enormity of the earthquake and tsunami, which caught Japan by surprise.

The tsunami smashed into the town of Natori, in Miyagi Prefecture, with waves that were three stories tall.

Chapter 4
Tsunami Hits the Shores

At 2:49 p.m. local time on March 11, three minutes after the earthquake struck, the Japan Meterological Agency issued three warnings about the tsunami that was on its way. The warnings predicted tsunami waves measuring ten feet (three meters) or more in height. In fact, the waves were more than thirty-three feet (ten meters) high and were more than four times that height in some places. One survivor recalled, "It was as if the tsunami fell from the heavens."

The vastly underestimated height of the water, along with the fact that such enormous tsunamis are extremely rare, caught people off guard. In addition, some didn't take the tsunami warnings seriously, some assumed that seawalls would keep them safe, and others didn't understand that tsunamis have intervals of lower water. For a range of reasons, many thousands of people were swept away by tsunami waves so suddenly that they had no chance of reaching safety. Others watched in horror from high locations as their towns and fellow citizens were overtaken by the water. The hardest-hit areas were Iwate, Miyagi, Fukushima, and Ibaraki **prefectures**, all of which are located along the northeast coast of Honshu.

Ishinomaki, Miyagi

Ishinomaki, in Miyagi Prefecture, is a city of roughly 160,000 people located at the north end of Sendai Bay. It was among the locations hardest hit on March 11. Close to half of the city was inundated by the tsunami, with waves reaching as high as sixty-six feet (twenty meters). The city center was wiped out, and more than 50,000 buildings, including over 20,000 homes, were destroyed or damaged. Streets were filled with crushed shops, houses, and fishing boats.

More than 3,500 of Ishinomaki's residents lost their lives—more than twice as many as in any other city or town in all of Japan. Ishinomaki Okawa Elementary School was one of the many public schools totally destroyed. About two-thirds of its students and teachers were swept away while crossing a bridge to reach higher ground.

Survivor Account

Nobukazu Endo, a piano tuner who was involved with Ishinomaki's music scene, was overwhelmed at first by the scale of the devastation in his city. He thought Ishinomaki could never recover from such an enormous disaster. Before long, however, he came up with the idea of organizing a large outdoor charity concert as part of a recovery effort. He said, "I'd like the rest of the nation and the world to know that Ishinomaki is going to be OK, that we'll survive."

Survivors had a tough time in the aftermath of the tsunami. The death toll rose steadily, and thousands were missing and unaccounted for. Roughly 18,000 residents who lost their homes were living in temporary shelters. A large number of the survivors needed medical care, but Ishinomaki Municipal Hospital as well as numerous clinics were destroyed or shut down. Many patients at Ishinomaki Red Cross Hospital were ill with **hypothermia** or pneumonia as a result of being immersed in water for hours, and many died. Another health concern was the lack of sanitation, which increased the risk of disease.

Rebuilding Ishinomaki is a lengthy process that will take repairing roads, bridges, and other structures as well as constructing new housing, especially for people still living in temporary housing. Many residents lost their shops and had to move away in order to find work. Those who stayed are making an effort to restore hope to Ishinomaki.

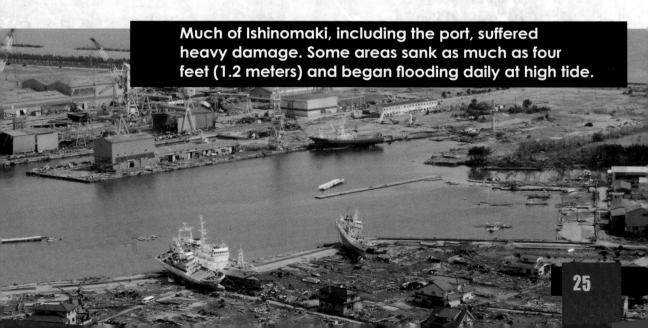

Much of Ishinomaki, including the port, suffered heavy damage. Some areas sank as much as four feet (1.2 meters) and began flooding daily at high tide.

Rikuzentakata, Iwatei

Rikuzentakata, a town in Iwate Prefecture that formerly had a population of about 23,000, lost the second-highest number of residents on March 11. When the tsunami warning alarm sounded, many people made their way to **designated** gathering places, including the city hall, a local gym, and a community center. Those locations had been established years before in anticipation of ten-to thirteen-foot (three-four-meter) tsunami waves, but the monstrous waves that inundated Rikuzentakata that day measured up to forty-nine feet (fifteen meters).

Roughly one thousand people gathered in the three buildings, and only one hundred survived. Most of them had managed to reach the third floor of city hall; the floors below that level were completely flooded, as was true of every building in town. The tsunami devastated Rikuzen-takata so completely that a newspaper article described the town as having been "wiped off the map."

The town of Rikuzentakata was nearly leveled, with damage estimated at $1.5 billion.

Survivor Account

Chihiro Kanno was at a practice session of her high school swimming team when the March 11 earthquake struck. Following established evacuation procedures, she and the rest of the team went to Rikuzentakata's community center. Tsunami waves carried Chihiro and a friend into a small storeroom. She tried to hold onto her friend's hand, but the force of the water was too strong. Chihiro survived in a small pocket of air, but her friend was swept away, along with six other teammates. Swimming helps Chihiro cope with the tragedy. "When I am alone, I cannot help thinking about my friends who died. When I am swimming, my friends are with me, we train hard together. I don't have to think about anything. I just empty my mind."

More than 1,500 people lost their lives, and nearly every structure in town was destroyed. The tsunami waves also flooded rice fields outside of town and swept uphill into mountain villages three miles (five km) from the shoreline.

The town's seawall had been damaged two years earlier by an earthquake, and the local fire chief warned his superiors that a tsunami could devastate the town. On March 11, the harbor gates didn't close properly before the tsunami hit the shore, and forty-five firefighters were swept to their deaths while trying to close the gates manually. Along the entire east coast of Honshu, a total of 284 firefighters died.

Recovery efforts in Rikuzentakata have been slow. Thousands of residents were still living in temporary housing three years later.

Minamisanriku, Miyagi

Minamisanriku is a town of about 17,000 in Miyagi Prefecture, only sixty miles (ninety-seven km) north of Sendai and very close to the earthquake's epicenter. In the immediate aftermath of the disaster, up to 10,000 people were feared dead, and reports speculated that ninety-five percent of the town had been destroyed. As in many other cities and towns along Honshu's eastern coast, people had not experienced such an enormous tsunami and never expected the water to reach nearly as high as it did.

Of Minamusanriku's eighty designated evacuation sites, more than thirty were completely inundated by the tsunami,

Survivor Account

Akiko Kosaka, a student from Minamisanriku, was attending a California university when her hometown was devastated by the tsunami. She feared that her entire family was lost. An email brought the news that her younger sister was safe in a school shelter, but Akiko was terrified that her parents, grandparents, and older sister had not survived. She cried for several days until a friend in Japan notified her of a very short YouTube video of Akiko's family home, still standing, amid a great deal of rubble. In the video, Akiko's older sister held up two signs with Japanese words. One said, "Kosaka Family," and the other said, "We are all safe."

killing everyone present. A high school teacher described the devastation by saying, "The entire town was simply swept away. It just no longer exists." A local reporter posted on Twitter: "10,000 ppl missing. horrible, whole town is gone. highway broken into bits, in mud, all mud, all gone. Incredible devastation, all buildings except hospital are gone, highway in pieces, only 3 buildings standing, hospital, some wedding place and one more building. rest are gone."

Mayor Jin Sato was among the ten town hall employees out of 130 who survived. Close to three-quarters of the patients in Shizugawa Hospital lost their lives, and almost 200 staff members survived only by climbing on the roof. The tsunami orphaned large numbers of children, whose schools were on high ground, while their parents were in lower locations. A young woman named Miki Endo saved many lives but lost her own by continuing to announce "Please run away fast" over the city's loudspeaker system until tsunami waves overtook the building she was in. In the end, Minamisanriku lost about 1,300 residents.

Only a few tall buildings were left standing in Minamisanriku in a sea of brown mud, including the hospital (back, center).

Sendai Airport

Sendai Airport was directly in harm's way because the earthquake's epicenter was eighty-one miles (130 km) east of the city of Sendai. The earthquake itself caused twenty-two cracks that ran the full width of runways and taxiways. It also caused shifting and sinking in certain areas that were built on top of sandy material.

In addition to earthquake damage, the entire airport, including taxiways and runways, was under water after tsunami waves up to fifty feet (fifteen meters) high came ashore. Many people escaped the water by climbing onto the roof of the passenger terminal or by entering the control tower, but aircraft, cars, trucks, and nearby houses were washed away, and electrical equipment was rendered inoperable. In addition, a fire burned in a passenger terminal. A day later, the airport was still submerged under eight feet (2.4 meters) of water, which left huge amounts of gravel and soil when it receded. Roughly 1,300 people were stranded in the terminal for two days.

To begin cleaning up the airport, a U.S. Air Force Special Operations team parachuted into a nearby town and proceeded to the airport by land. The team assisted Japan Self-Defense Forces in cleaning up enough debris that aircraft could fly in with supplies, equipment, and additional

Survivor Account

Kumi Onodera, a dental technician, compared Sendai after the earthquake and tsunami to "a scene from a disaster movie." She reported that the earthquake caused the ground to ripple. "The road was moving up and down like a wave. Things were on fire and it was 'snowing' [debris and ash]." Kumi said that it was difficult to stay positive when faced with such massive devastation. "You come to appreciate what you have in your everyday life. Everything is so hard now."

help. After further cleanup, which included moving over 5,000 automobiles that had washed onto the runway, the airport became a hub for distributing food, water, and blankets to people in the area. Air Force Major John Traxler, who directed aircraft while the airport's control tower was being repaired, said, "I have never seen this level of devastation, not even in combat." Sendai Airport reopened for commercial flights one month after the earthquake and tsunami.

Sendai, though hard hit in 2011 (below) and 1978 quakes, has become a leader in preparedness.

Kamaishi, Iwate

Kamaishi is a small, hilly city of about 40,000 people in Iwate Prefecture. Prior to March 11, one of its claims to fame was the Kamaishi Tsunami Protection **Breakwater**, a structure 6,400 feet (1,950 meters) long and 207 feet (63 meters) deep that reached almost twenty feet (six meters) above the water. Completed in 2009 at a cost of close to $1.6 billion, the breakwater took thirty-one years to construct and was listed in the Guinness World Records as the world's deepest breakwater.

The enormous seawall was no match for the March 11 tsunami, which crumbled it as the first thirty-foot (nine-meter) wave reached Kamaishi. In addition, water bouncing off the structure is believed by some residents to be

U.S. Urban Search and Rescue units helped look for survivors through structures and debris on March 16, 2011, in Kamaishi, Japan.

the cause of waves twice as large that destroyed two of Kamaishi's northern communities. More than 1,000 people in Kamaishi lost their lives that day or were missing. Many, mistakenly thinking the breakwater would protect them from harm, ignored the evacuation warnings broadcast throughout the city on loudspeakers.

Another safety strategy was far more successful. Almost all of Kamaishi's students—including those not in class-rooms—survived the tsunami, thanks to a tsunami disaster prevention education program developed by Toshitaka Katada, a disaster prevention expert and civil engineering professor at Gunma University, outside of Tokyo. The program focused on classroom activities that taught children how to take the initiative to save their own lives. The success of that program on March 11 has been referred to as the "Kamaishi Miracle."

Survivor Account

Many students in Kamaishi were with parents or other adults who didn't take the threat of a tsunami seriously after the earth-quake struck. The adults thought their locations were safely outside the danger zone, but the students remembered what they'd learned in class and urged everyone run to one of the city's evacuation routes, which would take them high above the city. The students saved not only their own lives, but also the lives of relatives and friends—by warning them and, in some cases, by carrying younger children or elderly people who were unable to move fast enough on their own. One boy said, "This is something we did all by ourselves. I don't think it's a miracle. It's an accomplishment."

Black smoke and white steam billowed over the Fukushima nuclear power plant for days as meltdowns and explosions continued.

Chapter 5
Nuclear Power Meltdown

Athird disaster took place on March 11 in addition to the earthquake and tsunami. Tsunami waves damaged the Fukushima Daiichi Nuclear Power Station (called "1F" in Japan) and created an extremely dangerous situation.

Before the Tohoku earthquake, about thirty percent of Japan's electricity was generated by nuclear power. When the earthquake struck, all nuclear reactors operating at the time in the region, including three units at 1F, shut down automatically, as they're designed to do. However, even a nuclear reactor is shut down, it must be cooled, as heat continues to be generated over an extended period of time.

Close to an hour after the earthquake, tsunami waves as high as forty-nine feet (fifteen meters) flooded 1F, causing a power outage that disabled most of its backup generators as well as pumps for cooling the reactors. As a result, the three reactors began to overheat. Despite site workers' desperate, nonstop attempts to restore cooling to the reactors, the overheated reactors underwent meltdowns. Heat, pressure, and **radioactivity** built up in the units' containment vessels, which eventually lost leak-tightness, leading to the release of an extremely large amount of radioactivity into the atmosphere. As a result, local residents within twelve miles (twenty km) of 1F were forced to evacuate the area, and close to 160,000 people in total evacuated out of safety concerns. A large amount of water **contaminated** with radioactivity also spilled into the sea due to the accident, leading to contamination of fish near the site. Because of the atmospheric and oceanic release of radioactivity, the 1F accident was rated as a level 7 (major accident) on the International Nuclear and Radiological Event Scale.

Survivor Account

Site workers faced grave dangers as they struggled to control the crisis at Fukushima Daiichi. Hundreds of workers stayed at the site for several weeks without going home at all. Many were local residents of Fukushima who had lost their houses and family members. Masao Yoshida, the site superintendent for Fukushima Daiichi, is credited with motivating site workers to do their best to stabilize the nuclear reactors. In describing the critical dangers that he and the other site workers faced, he said, "At that time, I was conjuring up faces of fellow colleagues who would die with me." Shift manager Ikuo Izawa stated, "I was determined to stay behind to my death; however, I was resolved to send my men back home alive." Another worker recalled, "Unit 3 could explode anytime soon, but it was my turn to go to the main control room. I called my dad and asked him to take good care of my wife and kids should I die."

Fukushima Daini (2F), the "sister" nuclear power station to 1F, was also heavily impacted by the tsunami, and three out of the four reactors lost the ability to remove heat from their respective containment vessels. However, the power supply survived the earthquake and tsunami, and site workers were eventually able to bring all of 2F's reactors to a safe and stable condition.

The March 11 earthquake also caused massive damage to the entire power supply system, leaving four million households in the greater Tokyo area without power for a few days. Rolling power outages occurred for ten days afterward.

Nuclear Power Stations

Nuclear power stations generate electricity by harnessing the energy inside atoms. Much of the process is the same as with coal-fired power plants: boiling water produces steam, which causes turbine generators to spin, which produces electricity. The difference is where the heat to boil the water comes from. Nuclear power stations produce heat by splitting atoms of uranium in a process called fission.

During this process, the atoms emit neutrons that cause additional fission to occur, called a "nuclear chain reaction." This reaction takes place in nuclear reactors in a controlled manner. A coolant, usually water, flows past the reactor core and absorbs the heat generated during fission, turning into steam. This steam is used to generate electricity.

The Fukushima disaster prompted widespread opposition to nuclear power among Japan's citizens. All of the country's forty-eight nuclear reactors had been shut down by late 2013. As a result, Japan has relied on more costly fossil fuel imports. **Decommissioning** 1F, decontaminating the offsite area, and compensating the afflicted people continue to be massive challenges. Controversy exists about whether to permanently abandon nuclear energy or resume with additional safety measures in place.

Message from Emperor Akihito

On March 16, Japan's Emperor Akihito addressed his nation's citizens on television to encourage them not to abandon hope. At the time, site workers at Fukushima Daiichi were struggling to contain the damage, and communities along the northeastern coast of Honshu were just beginning to grapple with the devastation caused by the earthquake and tsunami. Public appearances by a Japanese emperor are unusual, generally occurring only during a war or severe crisis. Emperor Akihito stated, "I hope from the bottom of my heart that the people will, hand in hand, treat each other with compassion and overcome these difficult times."

After the Fukushima disaster, many people in Japan protested against nuclear power.

Rescue workers and equipment were sent to help from all over Japan and the world.

Chapter 6

Consequences of the Disaster

The earthquake, tsunami, and nuclear disaster wreaked an incomprehensible amount of devastation. More than 15,800 people lost their lives; about 95 percent of deaths were caused by drowning, and none were due to radiation. Several thousand bodies were never recovered.

The earthquake and tsunami damaged or destroyed more than 1.2 million buildings. More than 4,000 roads were damaged, as well as bridges, railway facilities, factories, and commercial establishments. Most of the area's fishing boats were lost, and inundated farmland was damaged by salt from seawater. Electric power, communications, and water and sewer systems all suffered major disruptions. Estimates of direct economic loss from the earthquake and tsunami range from $200 billion to $309 billion.

An estimated 340,000 people were displaced by the disaster. Many emergency shelters were unsanitary and lacked sufficient food, water, and medicine, and many people died. Large numbers of rescue workers and military personnel in Japan were mobilized to help, and many countries and organizations around the world also provided assistance.

Far-Reaching Consequences

The Tohoku earthquake was powerful enough to impact conditions around the world as well as in space. It caused peculiar waves to slosh onto the shores of Norwegian fjords. Seismic waves caused the Whillans Ice Stream, a fast-moving river of ice in Antarctica, to flow faster. The European Space Agency's GOCE satellite, orbiting at roughly 160 miles (260 km) above Earth, detected low-frequency sound waves from the earthquake.

The tsunami also affected areas far beyond Japan. At Midway Atoll National Wildlife Refuge, a tsunami wave killed more than 110,000 nesting seabirds. About seven hours after the earthquake, waves reached the shores of Hawaii and Alaska, and they later hit California, Oregon, Washington, and British Columbia as well as the coast of Chile. Tsunami waves eventually traveled 8,000 miles (13,600 km) to Antarctica, where they caused close to fifty square miles (130 km^2) of icebergs to calve from the Sulzberger Ice Shelf.

Another consequence of the tsunami was a staggering amount of marine debris. When the waves receded, they carried cars, boats, household items, shipping containers, fishing equipment, and collapsed houses back into the ocean. An estimated 3.5 million tons of heavier debris sank close to Japan's shoreline. Roughly 1.5 million tons of floating materials were carried out to sea, originally consolidating in debris fields around Japan and eventually dispersing while crossing the ocean on their way to the west coast of North America. Marine debris is hazardous to wildlife because of the risks of entanglement, the potential for transporting invasive species, and the ingestion of plastics, which can allow harmful chemicals to enter the food web. Debris fields can also be a navigational hazard and a threat to human health and safety, and can harm the environment. Government agencies are working with local communities to address the problem.

Shifting the Planet

The Tohoku earthquake was powerful enough to impact the entire planet. According to NASA geophysicist Richard Gross, Earth has been spinning faster since March 11, 2011, and an Earth day is 1.8 microseconds shorter than it was prior to the enormous seismic event because Earth's mass was redistributed. The earthquake also shifted the planet's figure axis—the axis around which its mass is balanced, not its north-south axis—by about 6.5 inches (17 cm). As a result, Earth wobbles a little differently than it did before. Commenting on the shifts, Gross stated, "These changes in Earth's rotation are perfectly natural and happen all the time. People shouldn't worry about them."

Recovery

Japan is struggling to recover from the 2011 disaster. Many communities were fractured, and almost 270,000 people were still displaced three years later. Coastal rebuilding has been slow, and certain areas around Fukushima Daiichi continue to be designated as **mandatory exclusion zones** due to **residual** radiation. Displacement and trauma have taken a heavy toll. The Japanese government is spending $250 billion on a five-year plan to reconstruct the northeastern coast of Honshu, but the task is monumental and progress is slow.

Large earthquakes continue to affect Japan, including the magnitude 7.3 Kamaishi earthquake in December 2012. These seismic events are sobering reminders that earthquakes and tsunamis are enduring realities for this island nation.

The fact that more people didn't die on March 11, 2011, is a testament to the Japanese people's achievements in earthquake and tsunami preparedness as well as their collective dedication to action and innovation in the face of challenges. The fact that close to 20,000 people did lose their lives is prompting widespread efforts to learn from the disaster. These efforts include investigating improvements in earthquake and tsunami prediction, early-warning systems, disaster prevention education, and assistance for the survivors of these colossal forces of nature.

Wearing masks because of all the debris in the air, disaster survivors began to start over.

Glossary

breakwater A barrier built along a coastline to protect a harbor or coast from the force of waves.

contaminated Made dangerous or dirty by adding something polluting, poisonous, or otherwise harmful.

convection A series of circular movements that occur in substances when heat is transferred as hotter material rises and colder material sinks repeatedly.

debris Scattered pieces that remain after something has been destroyed.

decommissioning Officially removing something, such as a nuclear reactor, from service and making it safe by dismantling and decontaminating it.

designated Assigned a certain status to.

devastating Causing ruin.

displaced Forced to leave one's home or community; caused to be shifted from a usual location or area.

epicenter The point on Earth's surface directly above where an earthquake originates.

evacuation The act of removing people from a dangerous area.

exclusion zone An area into which entry is not permitted.

fault zone An area of fracture caused by the movement of tectonic plates.

hydraulic Operated by water or another liquid moving under pressure in a confined space.

hypocenter The point within Earth's crust where an earthquake originates.

hypothermia The condition of having a dangerously low body temperature.

inundated Covered with an enormous amount of water; flooded.

mandatory Required by laws or rules.

megathrust Related to an exceptionally powerful type of earthquake that occurs at a subduction zone.

meltdown An accident in which a nuclear reactor's fuel rods overheat, melt, and release radiation.

prefecture Any of the districts that Japan and certain other countries are divided into for the purpose of local governance.

radioactivity Rays of energetic particles that are spontaneously emitted when the nuclei of certain elements disintegrate.

residual Remaining after most of something is no longer present.

For More Information

Books

Buck, Pearl S. *The Big Wave.*
New York: HarperCollins Publishers. Reprint edition, 1986.

Hawkins, John. *Tsunami Disasters*. New York, NY:
Rosen Publishing, 2012.

Roza, Greg. *Powerful Earthquakes*. New York, NY:
Gareth Stevens Publishing, 2012.

Websites

Because of the changing nature of Internet links, Rosen Publishing has
developed an online list of websites related to the subject of this book. This
site is updated regularly. Please use this link to access this list:

http://www.rosenlinks.com/SD/Japan

Index